15 Ways to Heal the World

Lucy Rowella Tibbits

First Published in 2012 by:
New Lime Publishing
www.newlimepublishing.com

ISBN 978-0-9571267-7-0

Written by the hand which guides me
for my beautiful Katia

With sincere love to all that have joined me at some stage of my journey; for all the Experiences, the Learning, and Wisdom we have gained together.

Especial gratitude to Victoria xxx

Inspiration

A few months ago, I woke one morning to find a sentence scribbled on a piece of paper beside my bed. As I began to tune into the day, I had a vague recollection of being jolted awake in the middle of the night with a profound phrase in my head, which I remember feeling compelled to write down. It took many days to comprehend the intensity of this message, but I knew at once that it was a Gift, a piece of Spiritual Wisdom which had been sent to me, and which would be the essence of the book which I would consequently write:

"Life is just a flicker of consciousness in the Universe..."

15 Ways to Heal The World

Contents

Introduction

What are we, if not particles of planetary mass, making our way through the Universe? Why do we continue to grow as we do? Ever expanding, multiplying: mutating within the hands of God. We place all our happiness within our own hearts yet I watch the future in an image I hold somewhere in my memory. Or is it a vision? Many psychologists dismiss the concept of consciousness as an immeasurable, abstract by-product of the brain's activity. But if we were to dismiss all we could not logically assess, where would that leave us? Pounding the walls of a clinical white box, striving to break free and breathe in the scent of the wet earth, the pounding of the rain on the heat of our passion.

To dismiss the soul is to dismiss the enormity of human existence: The tears shed at dawn for the virgin sun; the burning embers of sunset pouring sweet pain through our hearts; the agony of music speaking through blissful chords to a deeper force. The hand which guides mine and creates the words of poetry, the images of paint, the words in this book - who is this if not my soul - or the spirit of another? It's the energy which resonates through the bark, which quivers beneath the earth, which touches the soul with gentle caress.

If our physical makeup is planetary mass, then what is our soul if not a tiny fragment of God?

Part One

“OURSELVES”

1: Redefine Prosperity

"If we invested as much of our daily lives into beautifying the Soul as we do the body, what glorious human beings we could be..."

Sometimes it is in suffering materially that we are handed the gift of spiritual evolution. Often in our quest for material survival in the hardest and most financially depleted of times, we come to find the essence of who we truly are within our souls and as we begin to nurture this discovery, we set ourselves free to experience life from the Soul. Eventually we no longer feel the need to cling to the fragile and temporary security of financial prosperity, but to embrace the completeness of total spiritual grounding: prosperity in its highest form.

At first this may seem a far cry from what is attainable and real in the contemporary western world. But it is not. It is real. Why succumb entirely to the pressure of material possession, when you can set yourself free from the spiritual wasteland and nourish the soul with the beautiful free gifts of the world?

We can be prosperous in the quality of moments we have immerse ourselves in our passions: painting, playing music, sinking our hands into the earth and watching new plant life grow. Prosperity is the beauty of being alive; of sharing time with children. It is in the moments lost beneath the stars; in the rain upon our faces and the wind in our hair. We find prosperity in our physical health and through our emotional wellbeing. Prosperity comes in the form of knowledge, in the energy of learning. It is in the ability to shine, in the talents which define who we truly are. Prosperity is in the ability to laugh freely; it is the acceptance of faith.

We can be prosperous in the quality of the relationships we nurture; the love shared between friends, the moments of trust which develop psychically between individual souls. We can be prosperous in the acceptance of our sexuality, in loving honestly, without boundaries of shame and obligation. We can be prosperous in the freedom to live with joy, not suspended in hope or regret but to simply live. Find it in the moments of simply being.

This is not to suggest that we all throw in our jobs and spend the rest of our days drifting about in a lifestyle which does not meet our personal level of ability. On the contrary, when we know and respect our true Soul, we want to work hard at what we do, because it is a part of who we truly are. We need to pursue that which is innately important within us. We need to unearth the gifts which we possess, which we can pass on to those around us, and that is not necessarily the highest paying or the most financially affluent job.

This is the path which will lead to the deepest level of long-term prosperity. Maybe this sounds unattainable in the "real world". The truth is, however, that the so-called "real world" to which we so cynically refer, is a social construction which is being created on a daily basis by the framework of the western materialist culture. At the level of the Soul however, everything in the world around us is real in every second of every single day. The passionate love affair is as actual as the long and practical marriage; the glorious picnic under the stars belongs as much in the real-world as the hard-slog overtime on a Friday night.

In truth, the world evolves from the way in which we choose to create it. All we have surrounds us and we view this through whichever lens we choose. This is far from being an effortless, fancy-free task. On the contrary, it is the reflection of a courageous journey into the Soul; a challenging of boundaries set by contemporary society that happiness is defined by possessions and that status is defined by money. It's having the spiritual valour to discover the fire in the Soul to shout to the world in whichever way we choose: "this is me!"

But if the ultimate in prosperity is true peace and soul happiness, why do so many of us force ourselves to sacrifice this perfect, attainable gift in pursuit of prosperity in its most superficial and fragile of forms?

Now ask yourself again, from the spaces inside your Soul: what is the true meaning of prosperity?

2: Nurture the Child Within

"Strive for the Mind of an adult...the Spirit of an elder...and the Soul of a lissom child..."

Delight is an emotion which very few of us can truly claim to experience as we get older. It's happiness in its absolute purest and most exquisite form. Delight is happiness which is untainted by cynicism, unaffected by past experiences or future anticipation. Delight is not governed by hope or driven by desire; neither is it quelled by fear or diluted by anticipation. Delight is a moment of total immersion in joy; in experiencing a moment right there, right now. Delight is the breath of life itself right there in the palm of our hands, on the tips of our fingers, deep down in the bottom of our hearts. How wonderful it would be to discover delight in our worlds once again, if only in the smallest of moments.

As I write this I am sitting in the harbour at St Ives, Cornwall; watching the boats on a harbour. The surrounding houses let the world wash by with the steady, innate wisdom that enlightens pure joy. "The light in St Ives": it's such a cliché but it's become so for a reason. It's the kind of light which takes everything it touches into an ethereal other-world; the afterglow of and late summer sunset dripping through a corn field. Yet it's only April. Early spring: a time of fresh beginnings. St Ives will never be new. It is ancient and wise and eternal. It's a hidden truth, a wisdom which unfolds before me. Every time I come it shows me something new about myself: something I was hiding from, or something I never even knew.

I'm watching Katia play in the sea, three months short of her fifth birthday. She has bonded with a group of other children. They're busily building a wall to stop the sea from coming in too far. They have such faith in themselves, such belief that they can defy even the inevitable power of the tides: she and her band of kindred spirits who, until this moment of sharing, were strangers.

What we stand to learn from such beautiful faith! I pray that I won't crush her spirit, or try to make her me; that I'll clip her wings or try to box her. Hold this moment forever in your spirit my angel: let your spirit grow ancient but may your soul remain forever a child: free, open and believing.

My Promise

If you falter from your path
I comfort you.
If spring becomes deep winter
I weep for you.
If shadows prey upon your heart
I bathe you in moonlight.
If your beautiful light should fade to black
I rest with you.

Baby

Wonder and promise shine in your eyes
Like droplets of delicious starlight.
On silent wings through deepened skies
Will dreams and wishes come to you.
Day by day your heart will come to know
The tiny flame of life that burns within you.
And with each breath, your perfect soul will grow
And you will become the gift that God has sent you.

...June 2005

My Child

The scent of petals hangs, heavy and soporific
In the aqua glow of dusk.
Scent, like sacred balm.
The sensual depths of Indian Wisdom
Healing like candlelight on a deep lagoon.
Still droplets of Holy Water,
Sensuous and complete:
So I hold you in the palm of my Spiritual Hand.
My Sacred Jewel from the Great Beyond.

... June 2005

3: Make Friends with your Shadow Self

"It's in embracing our darkness that we discover our true light"

It's through the acceptance of the almost incomprehensible eternity of the universe that we find the tiny flame of spirit which binds us with the universal consciousness, and which makes us who we truly are. The blissful delight is that nobody – not even the most learned – can yet fully answer the questions of existence.

According to Carl Jung, the shadow self is the unconscious part within all of us which consists of the base drives, undesirable qualities and negative traits which every human possesses to some degree, but which we are unwilling to accept. Jung's philosophy is that the only way to know and become our true self is to recognise, acknowledge and embrace the undesirable shadow self, integrating it into our conscious *reality, so that we may pass into the realms of the true essence of spirit.*

There are endless questions about the implications of a shadow self: social constructionists believe identity to be flexible and diverse; we create different identities according to the situation and surroundings and the role in which we are playing. From this angle, the concept of a "true" and "shadow" self are irrelevant. But what if self and identity are different sides of the same coin? Identity is social. Our tapestry of diverse subject positions and identities are as true as the hand which cast them. The shadow self, un-witnessed by observers, unknown even to oneself is one which is real and true. The true self, hidden at the centre of our concentric spiritual existence, is the part which connects with the Universe; the part which reads the message in the stars; touches the breath of an angel with fiery hands.

But to embrace this perfection, to swim in the delight of truly knowing our existence and suspension in the harmony of the universe, we must first know how it is to be human: To feel through pain and anguish, through eroticism and fear; through humiliation and control, the corruption of true understanding as viewed by the eyes of convention. In the concrete world, the brightest light casts the darkest shadow. The bleached white building which presses itself to the midday sun throws a short but intensely dark shadow. Yet as the day begins to wane, the light becomes gentle and shadows fuse into the landscape; extensions of the figure which cast them.

In accepting the shadow side as part of the coherent whole, we can allow the resonance of the true self to glow beneath the shadows. Why should we strive for uni-polar perfection when in reality our souls exist as a perfect union of day and night, north and south, life and death– and all the layers of intrigue in between?

It's through the acceptance of the most incomprehensible eternity of the universe that we find the tiny flame of spirit which makes us who we are inside. The blissful delight is that nobody – not even the most learned amongst us – can answer the questions of existence.

In Moonlight

Do not be afraid, my love
To walk the path of your
Own private Mystery

Seek within the courage to be bold
To embrace the flame of Spirit
Which guides your private Destiny

Make peace, my love
With the darkness in your Soul
For every shadow casts its light
In the Harmony of the world.

Mad Woman

Every night her nails touch the fingertips of death
But every night the persistence of her life
Engulfs her like cancer.
Every dawn she reaps in the harvest of her own blood
With the thirst and passion of a hungry saviour.
Dutifully giving the Eucharist of insanity
To the array of voices she calls
Her Congregation.

Each grabbing hand, each wild eye, each mocking scream
Reaches out to touch their Maker;
And their Maker grabs the ropes to haul herself
Up the mast of Death:
Black sinews of hair across her ivory skull,
And the nails shred the sail
Slowly rotting and fraying over the bony rigging
In the Tempest of her Life.

...April 1997

“As I Am” acrylic/mixed media on canvas - 2011

4: Find Acceptance in the Here and Now

"Acceptance of where and how you are is the key to moving forward"

I'm sitting in a cafe, dwelling on the thought of another Christmas approaching where I'm not swept off my feet by romantic love; where I have little left of the overdraft and with the bleak realisation that not one of my new year's resolutions has been acknowledged in the past 11 months and 2 days. But as I watch an elderly woman dragging her reluctant limbs along the pavement to the beat of her dampened heart, I realise I merely have to shift the focus of my spotlight a little to encompass the richness of the world, which spirals outwards from my own private kernel of grief.

It dawns on me as I look out of the window and observe the flow of human existence, that I've spent my entire adult years waiting for something to happen: waiting for that big event that's going to change my life; that's going to make my life perfect and whole; that big event, which is going to make life happen. I sit back and observe the passage of time for a moment more: the woman in the corner tapping on her laptop.

Is she successful, has she made it? Or is a part of her soul crying out for love? Hopelessly surrendering to the noose of a painful union? Yearning for the gifts of freedom and light? The tender young man sipping coffee with the beautiful older woman: Is he truly at peace with the passion, the excitement, the adventure that he craves? Or is there a void inside his heart, desperate to be cherished in a way he was never embraced as a child? I see it in this moment of time: life doesn't happen to us on one blessed day. It is happening now. Right now; this is life, on this planet, in this dimension; just as it is. Right here before our eyes.

It's in the scent of white lilies, which pours like balm into my throat; the sensuousness of the hot chocolate between my lips. It's in the beauty of another; in the touch of a friend. It's in the unconscious passage of feelings and knowledge between people who truly connect. It's in the sad days which make you remember moments when you felt truly alive; times when in hindsight we come to realise that life was truly happening; perfect and complete; just as we have been waiting for.

Do we stop to notice that in these moments of harmony and bliss, this is IT? Or do they slip through our fingers like air, taken for granted until the harmony becomes discordant again? By constantly striving for what we don't have rather than loving with heart, mind and soul the abundance of gifts that we do, we begin to yearn for the freedom of simply being; a gift which we so rarely cherish whilst we have it there in our hands. In all of our lives, we need to stop and feel the moment. Breathe the moment. Bless our talents, our creativity. Adore the freedom to laugh, to run, to love and to play. Because this is Life; and it's happening now.

The whole concept of "going with the flow" and "being in the here and now" is often met with trepidation in western culture. In a society focussed so strongly on individualism and striving to surpass our material goals, there is understandably a tendency to misinterpret the concept of Acceptance as an act of complacency. It's a common misconception to think that this means we should be floating about in a constant meditative and emotionless void, never pushing ourselves beyond this comfort zone, never striving to better ourselves.

However, this could not be further from the truth. On the contrary, Acceptance is an active psychological and spiritual process, which takes a great deal of self- awareness and conscious engagement with the world around us. At times of emotional imbalance, unhappiness, fear, loneliness, there is a great tendency within us all to immerse ourselves into the luxury of reminiscence, planning or dreams.

When we take a moment to sit in quiet meditation and simply observe the myriad thoughts ricocheting through the mind, we realise how they are constantly shaping and reshaping the future, playing and re-playing the past, without really getting us anywhere. At this point we tend to give up, believing we have failed to reach that "in the moment" state of mind and that clearly going with the flow is not for us. However, this state of realisation is the vital starting point to unearthing the true state of our minds. If we can begin to objectively assess our own lives by gently unravelling the blanket of fantasies, memories and abstract thought which obscures and protects us from the truth: then we are going with the flow; then we are practicing Acceptance; and only then we can truly move onwards.

It takes great courage and faith to walk away from our obsessions and addictions, our damaging relationships, our unfulfilling occupations or our weary lifestyles, and to take a step onwards into the next phase of our spiritual journey here on Earth. It takes great strength and effort to train our thoughts away from the web of the past and images of the future, and to allow the current situation to truly become us, so that we can truly understand it and consciously act upon it.

Sometimes it's vital just to be where you are for a while; feel how you feel; do what needs to be done. Hanging onto the past and anticipating the future is resistance to change. Acceptance of where and how you are now is the key to moving forward.

5: Dance

"Love truly. Live deeply. Run free!"

Dance! Let the energy of freedom flow through your body. Dwell not on that which aches but dance with love for the body which carries your spirit through the glory of life itself.
Take delight in the air which slips between your fingers at night; tears through your hair by day; kisses your face as the rain beats down.

Adore the wet earth between your toes as you rejoice in the sense of touch present as a gift. Dance your dance in life; true to your Soul.

Drink in the scent of flowers, the dampness of wood, the warmth of the sun and sink deep into the glory of transportation to a memory, by the delicious sense of smell: the sensuality, the excitement; the key to every emotion, every memory; every lesson of your journey along the way.
Dance to the gentle breath of dawn, the colours in the virgin sun; the passionate opera of a sunset finale. Indulge in the architecture of spiders; the craftsmanship of bees.

Dance for the sheer bliss of being alive in a body which can move. Trust the soul to set you free, free to move in the dance of love; for adoration, for passion, for the sake of sensuality alone. Indulge in the touch of another; the scent of a lover; the dance of yearning and desire; the tender breath of love.

Dance with liberation! Embrace the pinnacle of reckless abandon like a horse set free in the waves. Feel the beat of the Earth racing through your heart.

Dance as though you only have your life to live.

"Ballerina" charcoal on paper - 1999

6: Achieve Inner Stillness

"When the Soul is at peace, the Spirit can fly"

Tai Chi can be a powerful journey into the soul through blissful acknowledgement of what the body can do. It brings joy through the freedom of movement with our own private sphere of energy, and connects to the Universal energy which binds us all with the Universe and with each other. I am no authority to offer guidance in the practice of tai chi, but rather to reflect on my own private learning and find the way in which to guide the spirit away from the day to day stresses into the kingdom of Light. My Light: the light of others around me, in which I dance and unite; the light of Guidance and purity, of passion and calm. Ultimately, it is the union of the light of Heaven and Earth, of simply acknowledging that we are, in this moment, boundless energy.

Alone, private dreamer, through your dance of sorrow; make way for the light to pick you up in glints of daybreak though your beat-down Soul. Life can become the time for you when you will truly feel who you are. Through the meditation of the Spirit, the binding of the energies which draw us inwards to our true essence, we find stillness.

Through the weapons, which we call love, we bond true sorrow with pure joy: the ecstasy of longing, the agony of bliss; binding energies from around our feet and from higher orders of consciousness.

Consciousness is all around us. We find it in the spaces between our fingertips; between the beats of our hearts. It's in the voids between the stars; the binding of the galaxies. It's the energy which keeps us all together, in our hearts, minds, bodies and souls. Through the binding of these energies, which we hold in the palms of our hands, we find the true meaning of Freedom.

In our hearts and minds, the dream of belonging becomes real. We are drawn into the light which surrounds us. Our Souls are connected with the Universal Consciousness from which we are created; to which we shall return. When the Soul is at peace, the Spirit can fly; set free to the pulse of the Earth

Stay with your stillness for a moment more
Breathe through your light with your heart and mind.
Open your spirit to the life beyond you,
Feel honesty pouring into your heart:
Be not that which you yearn for;
Strive not to attain that perfect grace;
Seek not to tie the boundaries around you,
But be still in the light that you are.
Simply be with your Self in this moment.
Do not try to dichotomize your life
By striving to find the true self within the complexities which surround us;
But simply accept the Whole as the way you are
And the Truth will rise like a Phoenix
From the ashes of your own courageous fire.

Part Two

"OTHERS"

7: Spend Precious Moments with Precious Others

"A kindred spirit is one who holds a mirror to your heart and helps you look inside"

The significant relationships in our lives provide passwords to the passages leading to our enlightened Truth. They can serve to deepen the understanding which lies at the level of the Soul, and to introduce us gradually to the fullness of our own Shadow Self.

The significant relationships in our lives provide mirrors to our own Soul. Often what we perceive as a "bad" relationship is, at the subconscious level, a distorted mirror image of our fears, our anxieties and our undesirable traits; those which we endeavour our lifetime long to conceal from our own conscious reality.

In our innate psychological pursuit of perfection we repeatedly project our negative traits onto the behaviour and countenance of others, allowing us to legitimately despise and chastise our Shadow Self by watching it play itself out over and again through the actions and words of others. Through the people who disturb or repel us, we seek to bury the shadow self further and further away from our own conscious mind. Therefore, often we are drawn to damaging relationships because they echo our own weaknesses and satisfy the negative beliefs we subconsciously maintain about ourselves.

Often it is through these "wrong" relationships that we embark upon the most profound and powerful stages of our Spiritual Journey. Every experience we encounter offers a gift of Learning, and it is with willingness to learn that we can acquire infinite Wisdom. In allowing ourselves to become receptive to these lessons and to have the courage and grace to release the earthly experience into this universal realm of acceptance and understanding, we become grateful for the presence of every significant relationship in our lives, regardless of whether the experience itself created gentleness, ecstasy, peace or love...or whether it fuelled jealousy, fear, anger, humiliation or pain.

Perfection is a challenge which can never be met, for every trait is bipolar, therefore in order to experience the pinnacle of beauty, we must also know its darkest opponent and to be willing to witness it there both within ourselves and through the eyes of others.

Especially in romantic relationships, people come into our lives to take on one of a myriad different roles, each one as much a miracle as the other yet incomparable in their diversity: the Twin Soul, the Rescuer, the Grounding Force, the Liberator, the Guiding Light, the Teacher, the Playmate, the Destroyer, the Nurturer, the Follower, the Erotic Indulgence, the Spiritual Revelation...

However, the one to whom we feel most spiritually united is not necessarily the one with whom we can practically share a permanent partnership in this earthly life. However intense and complete the union on an ethereal level, it is vital to acknowledge where we are in this life, and to keep our feet firmly encased in the earth.

Twin souls can be like air and water, an indigo life-force, ethereally complete, yet lacking in the solidarity needed to balance the physical world. Water gets lost in water; Air dissipates into air; Earth crumbles into earth; Fire ignites fire beyond control. But often we come to learn that Air feels most beautiful when the feet are rooted in wet earth. Water sparkles its brightest beneath the moonlight when it rushes over pebbles; cups the sunset most eloquently when it rests heavily on a bed of stones. Fire holds enchantment and grace when contained within a bed of clay.

How does this reflect in our most significant relationships? Where does it resonate in the sharing of our journey on earth?

Look for the reflection of your Soul in others: a fragmented, distorted, mirror-mosaic image of the Self. Look closely enough with acceptance and faith, and you will catch the light of Truth in your own eyes, its expression holding you close, more intimate than you may wish to believe. Yet it is there when we behold it, and in doing so we find another sphere of completion within ourselves; through the Soul of another.

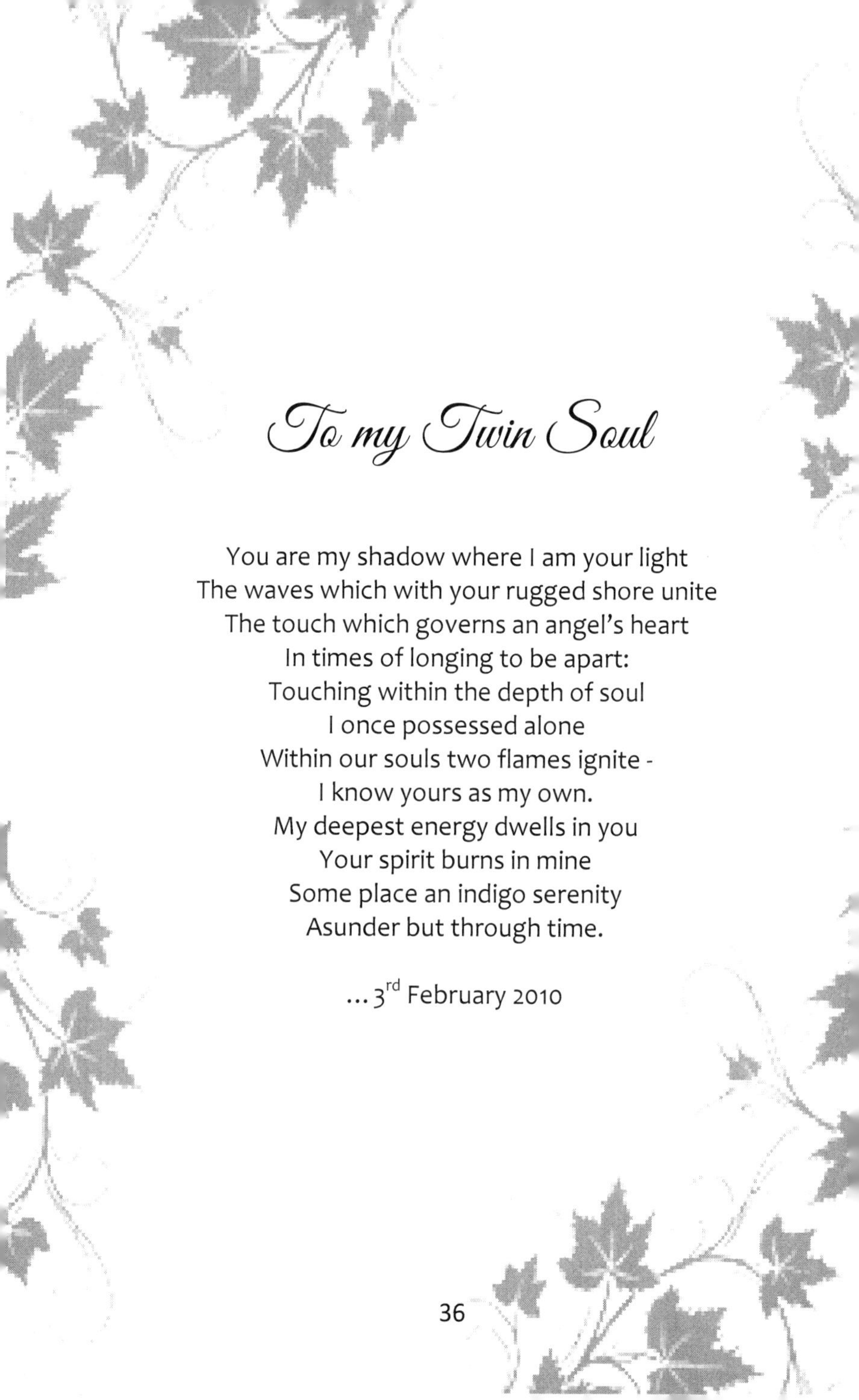

To my Twin Soul

You are my shadow where I am your light
The waves which with your rugged shore unite
The touch which governs an angel's heart
In times of longing to be apart:
Touching within the depth of soul
I once possessed alone
Within our souls two flames ignite -
I know yours as my own.
My deepest energy dwells in you
Your spirit burns in mine
Some place an indigo serenity
Asunder but through time.

... 3rd February 2010

8: Forgive an Old Hurt

"Life is an illusion: it depends on where you stand"

Imagine a house. It has been yours for as long as you can remember and you are wholly content and comfortable living there. One day, a faulty switch catches fire, and within minutes, your entire home has succumbed to the flames. At that moment all your energy is concentrated on putting out that fire and saving your precious home.

After a while the fire dies down and eventually goes out, but what is left are just charred remains of what was once your beautiful sanctuary, the place where you felt so secure, so happy. The external walls are still standing, but the home inside is destroyed.

You realise you have two choices now: you can either turn and walk away from the house and leave it derelict, where it will eventually become nothing but a pile of debris, or you can begin to restore it, piece by piece. It will take a long time – there is a lot of work to be done, but with perseverance and strength, and with the help of the right people, it can be done. And so you begin.

As you go along, you rediscover parts of the house, which have somehow managed to survive. You come across old relics you had almost forgotten about, polish away the soot and many of them are almost as new! At this point you start to rethink the house a little: maybe it would be better to move that window to another position, get a different view – maybe even a better one? And as for the colour schemes, the carpets – let's improve on those too! Find something brighter - more cheerful, more confident!

And so the work continues. Sometimes things run flawlessly and you achieve so much in such a short time, but inevitably, at other times there are moments of hopelessness and dead ends; there are times when hope is weak and energy is depleted. But someone, somewhere always manages to find a way forward.

Finally, one day, it is finished. You sit outside on your brand new terrace overlooking the hillside, and open a bottle of wine to share with everyone who has helped to renovate the house: the decorators, architects, designers, plumbers... right down to the stranger who somehow delivered the tiny message you needed just at that time to move on. It is still your home – it still feels like your home, but it is stronger, brighter and more beautiful than you had ever imagined a home of yours could be!

And what of the faulty switch? Well, it almost devastated everything, almost took away all you had, threatened to leave you with nothing but charred remains of something that once was beautiful. Of course you could choose to dwell on this damage for the rest of your life. Or you could choose to look upon this beautiful new home you have created as a result and secretly thank that faulty switch for starting things off. After all, the only thing it really managed to destroy in the fire was itself.

"So...?" acrylic/mixed media on canvas - 2010

9: Learn From One at Their Journey's End

"Leave hoof-prints in the earth and laughter in the rain; to starlight we return"

On a bitter winter's night, Katia and I stop to look at the stars. It is one of those moments which takes me to the realm of the Spirit: the immortal expanse where boundaries do not exist and time defies the world of human love. I wish I could send my soul to those spaces between the stars.

I ask her why the stars are there. Her reply is pure and logical: because people have died. How my soul craves such perfect understanding: the understanding of a child. When our own tiny sphere of consciousness dissipates back into the Universe: so we return to the stars. So are we at one with ourselves, with one another, with the ground we walk on, the air that we breathe; the great and boundless Universe which simultaneously contains us, drives us and creates us.

We walk on, immersed in this timeless moment of Universal consciousness. We become the spaces in between, where light and laughter fuse into one universal being; where darkness and hope merge into one exquisite unity; so serene, so great, so beautifully harmonious.

Life is just a flicker of consciousness in the Universe.

Sleep tight my tiny angel.
Be still within your deep cocoon.
May I bless you with peace and bathe you in tranquillity.
The future shines already in your eyes,
Yet the past is embedded on your tiny hands.
May the stars light the way for you
And the sun be your guiding hand.
May the wind be your song
And the oceans drive your spirit.
And I will cherish you, my darling angel,
Until we meet again.

...June 2005

Through your journey

Do not let me sleep tonight
Behold a magical darkness which surrounds me.
Suspended in the moon; crushed by the sea
Heralded by the light of a myriad stars
Pressing through your reality.

Speak to me through dreams
My Spirit Guide awakens with
The song of her guiding heart
Wisdom in the palm of her hand
She lights the way

Do not let me sleep tonight
But touch me with your spirit
Hold a mirror to my life and make me
Look inside.
I'm not afraid: I know my truth
And my mind bears token to show me

But I can't. The raw embrace
Is stronger than my life itself.

Do not let me sleep tonight
For fear that I will wake.

"Holme Beach" acrylic on canvas - 2009

Part Three

"THE SPACES IN BETWEEN"

10: Listen with your Soul

"By truly listening, we can truly be"

We have become so reliant on our visual sense and take the world so much for granted though relentless familiarity, that it is easy to slip away and fail to notice what is truly happening, both in our external surroundings and deep within our souls.

We are so attuned to using visual information to interpret our world; but listening – truly listening – can enable us to communicate with our environment at a different frequency and therefore to embrace it from a new perspective, leaving the soul open to absorb the energy of the earth and to exist within universal consciousness at an entirely different level.

By listening to the world and focussing on the sounds around us, we are brought immediately into the here and now. Without awareness of the present moment, the mind runs incessantly amok with thoughts of what has been, and with preoccupations with what is or is not to come. The mind is a constant film reel, playing over and over again. We become obsessed with our memories, addicted to our pre-occupations and it is very difficult to break away from this cycle and feel the present moment if we continue through this medium of communication with ourselves.

There is only so much that we as human beings can consciously attend to and process. Information that is not of immediate relevance and importance is filtered out and we focus only on that which we select. So if we are preoccupied with negative thoughts and selfish indulgences, we will naturally fail to notice the details of the present surroundings, which are equally real, equally important – equally a part of real-life. If we can somehow concentrate our minds on perceiving positivity, we can begin to filter out the rehearsed negativity and pre-occupations on which we have become fixated, and begin to experience, understand and ultimately know ourselves from a wider and far more encompassing perspective.

Ultimately we are pure energy therefore it follows that we have the capacity to be completely fluid in our thinking, in our being, in our daily interactions and synchronicity with others and the world around us. How then is it that we ignore so much of what is put there right before our hearts?
Listen as the day unfolds; listen beyond the traffic sounds to the synchronicity of birds; the symphony of the breeze seeking its way around the Earth's myriad contours.

Listen to the vibrant peace of nature; the healing vibrations of Universal energy, of which each individual being is an integral part; begin to hear the enormity of life as it sings to the harmony of the Earth. Listen to the melody of daylight; the motion of light glistening on water, touching the earth with a gentle caress.

When we truly listen to our world, we lose the incessant sound of unproductive thought; lose the noise of the mind challenging the body and chastising the soul; dispel anticipation of failure and success in a hypothetical world which has never happened and which maybe never even will.

As we truly listen to our world, we begin to clarify the way we think, the way we perceive; the way in which we behave. In attuning ourselves to the audible vibrations of the landscape we bring ourselves one step closer to the Harmony of the Universe.

"Lichtspiel im Wald" acrylic on canvas, 2003

11: Pause to Discover Beauty on the Doorstep

"Fog is just fairy dust waiting to be kissed by the sun"

How many times have you stopped to notice the kiss of dawn on the waking world; the transformation of a spider's web into an exquisite work of art? How each dewdrop balances with perfect precision on the tips of frozen blades of grass?

How many times have you stopped to feel the shaft of sunlight penetrate your heart; an expression of pure energy radiating within? Or watched the particles of dawn dance within its light?

How many times have you stopped to taste how the sunlight plays with dewdrops, weaving its energy in and out of the delicate threads of grass? Feel how it weaves through your own soul, touching on the stillness which resides within.

How many times have you noticed how autumn air carries the scent of burning wood, even without the presence of flames? Sensed the quivering promise of life beneath the frozen earth in winter? Marvelled and dreamed at the wonder of the eternal dance of nature: life and death, death and life...

It has been a particularly hard winter for this part of the world; yet it presented us with a gift to temporarily transform all of our lives and the energy between us, which people are still talking about now, almost four months later.

We woke one day to find the world around us had been blessed with a coating of hoar frost on every possible surface it could find, right down to the finest fibre of last year's leaves. An ethereal light had been cast: across the vivid blue sky, soft ochre sunlight softened every contour showing us a hint of the ethereal fourth dimension.

I stopped to marvel a cobweb which was strung across a waste paper bin outside the church. It had been so trustingly left, appearing as if from nowhere like a crop circle in the night, woven in love. These spider's webs must be all over the place yet in daily haste we seldom notice them, but now they are everywhere, illuminated by granules of dew.

People were noticing trees on the horizon, which nobody had ever seen before. Through this surreal light and perfect white highlighting across the world, new horizons were quite literally being opened up before our eyes. People were stopping in the street to talk to one other, to notice together the exquisite beauty of this new-look world. Everyone appeared as if enchanted by the frozen molecules of dew shimmering in the atmosphere like the finest, finest glitter-spray.

The day brought love and joy to eyes whose colour I had until now never taken the time to notice. Through the shared joy in the new world, people were cherishing the unconditional, universal bond which unites us all, yet which we rarely stop to consider.

How different the world looks in an unfamiliar light! How beautiful and full of promise could our own situations become if we were to place them in a new light, view them from a broader perspective?

One tree in particular stood out from the rest. It stood a little back from the others, reaching up to the sky, etching its twigs into the blue. In the centre of this pure white tree, a solitary black crow had landed, in perfect accordance with the laws of artistic proportion.

Together this created a complete expression of the melody of the human soul: through the acceptance and of this kernel of blackness into the pure white aura, a celebration of spiritual perfection, clarity and radiance was accomplished.

All matter is energy, vibrating to the harmony of the Universe. The delicacy and intricacy of the spider's tiny dream-catcher resonates to the same harmony as the vicious ocean. It's in the watery light of dawn, which stirs the world with an aura of delicate violet; the sensual redness of twilight skies, an inferno of light spreading across the earth. It's the same resonation that connects us with the Universe; to one another; to the very essence of our human spirit.

12: Embrace the Enormity of the Ocean

"In every hand is the ardour to destroy and the divinity to heal"

How can it be possible to sit on Kynance Cove at high tide and still believe ourselves to be atheists? It's the most passionate coastline, the most empowered sea, like one thrown to the verge of madness through an unrequited and eternal love; bound by the same unleashed fervour screamed out by Christ on the cross: a message in the sea. This is God. This is God – the Universe - flinging devastating power over the helpless, weak, terror-bound humanity which through its own arrogance attempts to own this planet. God is not goodness and meek. These waves, this wild, God-driven ocean can kill the body and heal the soul. This is the taste of Heaven: the gateway to the next dimension.

Wind ripped tides fuse day and night
Through restless skies, an ancient time
Passes before me.
A time before I knew the way my life would
Grow to unfold beneath the grave.

Wilderness creeps now before my watchful heart
Reaching out to no-one,
But content within its own irony.
Wrapped beneath a shroud of melancholy bliss
And ancient, eternal solitude.

...October 2009

13: Breathe Vitality through a Rainy Day

"Colours shine brighter when the skies are grey"

Deep November: the time for retreating into the hibernation period of our lives. Postures sink; spirits become grey; yet our winter is part of the natural earthly cycle. Without these grey blustery skies the spring our lives would have no significant vitality.

Leaves dance with liberation on the wind, free at last from clinging all these months to the tree. It reflects the journey through human life. Beginning as an indistinguishable foetus embedded within the mother, the leaf evolves from within the tree and becomes the fresh green childhood of spring. Gradually it changes and colours intensify until it reaches late summer, the time of sensuality and an increasing sense of independence and emerging freedom. True colours flourish. Gone is the stark green, the unity, the freshness of summer. The boundaries begin to soften a little; the light adds a sensuous overtone. And now, in winter, the leaf loses its physical vitality, and one by one, the power of the wind the invisible persuasion of the Universe entice them one by one from the tree to which they have clung so long.

And how they dance; free at last from the clutches of earthly reality. This too is the cycle of physical life. Likewise our bodies follow the same journey, but what if the soul can follow a different path? Be set free sooner to dance through the air, to rejoice in the motion of the wind; the harmony of the planets. To be truly liberated to carry the wisdom of winter within a body of spring.

The wind is an empowering force and I let my hair down to feel its fingers ripping through. It tries to take me but my feet remain grounded in the wet earth. Its chill cuts through and I marvel at the journey through the Universe as our planet pulls further and further away from the sun. And so we begin our own spiritual journey, uncontrollable by human force, into the deeper, colder parts of the Soul.

Embrace the power of the elements; engage with the freedom of the wind. The undesirable can soon become desired. The uncontrollable soon becomes the source of empowerment and joy. Rediscover the childlike feeling of the whole world belonging in the palm of your hand.

The autumn leaves always shine brighter when the skies are grey.

"Cotswold Storm" acrylic/mixed media on canvas - 2009

14: Learn the Moon

"Keep your mind in this world but stretch your soul to the stars"

Defy convention and seek beyond the boundaries of society that which is truly beautiful. I stepped out into the garden last night: two days lay between this moment and the full moon, with all the awakening promise that the lunar eclipse would bring.

There she hung, high above the frozen world, spreading her blue light across my garden. My secret corner of woodland normally buried in darkness unfurled seductively, secretly for the naked eye, just this once beneath the enchanted sky. Branches stretched out in partial ecstasy, reaching in to the cold throes of the Universe, just that tiny fraction more.

And so is revealed a new world; one which we are all yet to embrace; a light which touches the secret legend of the world in which we live. When the lights are gone and the world is sleeping there is freedom to return to the Pagan soul; to root the feet in the earth and send the spirit soaring beyond the stars.

It's no wonder our ancestors were so wise in the ways of astrology. There were no other sources of energy but the celestial bodies, the earth and each other; nothing to interfere with the natural rhythms of the universe. It's no mystery that they experienced feelings of spirituality, bliss, messages and premonition. They understood. And so it is that we need to re-establish our spiritual connections and the read the language of the Universe.

Dance to the journey of the ever-changing moon, that immense mystery of light, so solid, so real, so horrifyingly intense, yet so fluid, so serene, so gloriously female. It's that resounding majestic silence which surrounds her there, suspended within its own field of Universal Consciousness: it's the spaces in between.

15: Speak the Language of the Universe

"Truth is simply being"

The contours of the building almost seem to be pushing their way out of the earth. With florid mosaic columns and mystical golden domes you could be forgiven for thinking you've entered the realms of fantasy. But these mystical forms belong to the spa complex Rognor Bad Blumau in Styria, Austria designed by Friedensreich Hundertwasser (1928-2002).

Harmony between man and nature was the essence of Hundertwasser's vision. He detested straight lines and even surfaces and predictable regularity. Instead, gently curving walls, sinuous columns, and undulating floors became his trademark. He literally brought the glory of nature into his buildings by topping roofs with grass, describing it as a religious act, reconnecting the human being with nature and ultimately, with God.

The Main House at Rogner Bad Blumau is a sensuous three-dimensional mosaic of earthly tones and black contours, central to which is the spa consisting of 2700 square metres of the most energising and nurturing thermal water in Austria. At night behind the billowing steam, the illuminated buildings surrounding the pool stand ethereal and haunting. Floating beneath the stars, it becomes clear that Hundertwasser not only managed to achieve his vision of harmony between man and God, but he surpassed it.

Through his art, Hundertwasser strove to defy the structure of education and to herald the creative spirit within. Through his architecture, he strove to transcend the boundaries between existential materialism and the spiritual realm. Immersed in the water, the world is devoid of sound; surrounded by steam, the world is devoid of humanity. Between myself and the stars there is that same sacred space which stretches for billions of light years between these heavenly bodies which we perceive as dots of light before our eyes. So often we say how small and insignificant we feel beneath the expanse of Universe around us. But somehow floating here beneath the stars strips us of our material being; we lose our sense of physical form; our self-contained manifestation of experiences, relationships and emotions. Instead we become a part of this infinite expanse of Universe above; as though the soul is set free to re-unite in its eternal immensity with the Great Beyond.

I feel I know each star like I know the moon; like I know my own breath. It's the hand that guides my work as I paint late at night; the poems which flow from the darkness with the oblivion of acute spiritual awareness. These are times in our physical lives when we wonder at the realms of the Universe; never truly understanding where we fit, where we play our part.

The ancient Greek philosopher Pythagoras believed that the Universe was held together in sacred musical harmony, which he claimed he could actually hear: the Universe in perfect harmony, resonating within itself and beyond into the next dimension. The chord which resonates within the thread of light that hangs a dewdrop to a spider-web is the same harmony as that which suspends Jupiter and Saturn in perfect harmony with the Sun. All the hectic, the unrest, the worry we create in our material world is surplus to the overwhelming oneness which is the harmony of the Universe

If we really can connect so intrinsically with this universal energy, then maybe it is possible to transcend the physical and to move beyond the boundaries of time and space, which dictate the path of our physical existence: so may we become pure spiritual wisdom.

In the physical world there is no truth; only the perceptual impression which bears the watermark of our previous experience. Life is an illusion: we can merely construct the world according to the watermark of our earthly and spiritual experiences.

“Reincarnation” acrylic/mixed media on canvas – 2003